The Voyage of MOTLEY ONE

An assembly of articles written by Sally and Richard Hope

They describe stages of the voyage they made, with their three children, from England to New Zealand in a catamaran.

Presented as a prelude to the publication of the complete story of

MOTLEY ONE

FOR   SALLY

KERRY, MELANIE and SAMANTHA

TABLE OF CONTENTS

WE   WOULD   GO

A'ROAMING

BY   Sally Hope

My husband Richard still had six years to serve on a twelve year engagement as an officer in the British Royal Air Force when he began seriously to consider what he would do when released. We had then been married for five years, making an early start at twenty years old. Service life gave security and social status but a series of home postings had denied us the hoped for travel opportunities. Again posted within England, on a job which, though interesting and at times exciting, meant a lot of just sitting about, my husband was getting restless. Without qualifications for any civilian occupation it seemed time for him to begin spare time study. His new station was in the South of England and he left me with our four year old daughter Kerry in Yorkshire while he searched for a house. By day in the Search and Rescue helicopters, he flew low over the coastal areas and began to take an interest in the intense yachting activity. Off duty, living in the Service Mess, he had time to think of the future, and to read. He reread a book he had had for several years, by a New Zealander who left the Army, bought a boat, and sailed home single handed from England. The idea struck home; disinclined to study and unable to visualize himself in a routine life, Richard decided that when his time in the RAF was finished he too would buy a boat, and sail around the world, but not alone. On one of his visits home he told me of his plan; Kerry and I were to go to sea too. It seemed a long way in the future and I had more immediate problems on my mind; I agreed it sounded like a fine idea and temporarily forgot about it. These days Richard tells people that I spent the next five years hoping he would drop the plan. Perhaps if I had dug my heels in at the start he would have done so, but I allowed myself to be slowly started on the road to the sea. The project soon had foundation; our new home was found, five minutes walk from the beach. Following an earlier interest Richard had bought a house with a good sized garden, intending to grow vegetables he dug up half the lawn. Five years later it was put to grass again, never having yielded anything; boats had come into our lives. The husband of the first friend I made in the new community had a boat for sale; it was soon ours, small but safe. Richard wanted to get the feel of the sea by going out fishing. The first trip was an omen; the engine failed, the anchor wouldn't hold, my husband, father and brother-in~law were adrift, to he towed in ignominiously by a fishing boat. Undaunted Richard held to his notion. Early the next year we spent a week on the Broads, the inland water system resort with sailing craft and motor cruisers for hire on camping style holidays. Another omen; I was terrified on my first sail, Richard learning the hard way on Barton Broad, where Nelson learnt to sail. That summer our "little tub" gave Richard some fun on the sea but I didn't join him, our second child was on the way. One more for the crew did not alter things, Richard was ever more set on "the plan". He had done some travelling abroad and loved to see new places, he wanted so much to share that with me, for I had never been far from home. Service life was too secure, its limits prescribed, the prospect of voyaging with its independence, and satisfaction of achievement in reaching far off places by his own effort had great attraction. If a civilian occupation had offered appeal Richard could have found time to prepare for it, for his job consisted largely of sitting about, on call for rescue work, and this he enjoyed, but the inactivity, especially in the winter months was increasing his need of an active life. I could see all this very plainly, and understanding, could not say no, I wouldn't go to sea, knowing that to do so might well ruin things between us. There were still three years to go and I hoped that some other interest might take hold or that the abandonment of security would finally seem too much to face. But we began telling relatives and friends of the long term plans; Richard felt that having publicised them, he would feel less able to change his mind. Even that early we could see that it would become easier to turn back than go on. While the baby, Melanie, was small, Richard was sent to Aden for twelve months, unaccompanied. He missed us intensely and was furious at missing her development. Out there he read a lot more of other voyages in small boats and met some long distance sailors. The main recreation was dinghy sailing. Left at home I felt the separation hard to bear too and resolved that to avoid its repetition, I would go with him on his voyage. In letters we began to discuss details, as part of the future we had to look forward to when together again. At first we held hopes of being able to afford an older craft, spend three years on a world cruise, nothing less would do, and return to our house to settle down. That helped me immensely. I had come to love our home and the community we lived in. I delight in group activities, had joined the Women's Institutes and the amateur dramatic and operatic societies. Taking part in all the productions I had made many friends. Richard though he tried to be a civilian when off duty,was too often away, and being naturally retiring had no such interest. My oldest friend had come to live in the area, and with parents, sister and beloved grandmother not far away family ties were closer too. There was a lot for me to leave, Richard had little to hold him. The promise of eventual return to a normal life, roots behind me, allowed me to maintain, publicly at least, my enthusiasm for his plan. The heat and intense humidity of Aden aggravated a physical discomfort due to a minor medical condition and Richard was sent home after only nine months. As far as the Service was concerned he was fit now only for employment in England, ineligible for extension of engagement. I could no longer hope that the security of the Air Force would win and I knew he would not he deterred. His final posting was near enough to let us retain our house, by the sea. It was time to get a small cruising boat and begin serious training. "Miss Prim" was only 19 ft. long, with three berths and just enough room to sit upright. We moored her off Selsey where we lived, to be readily accessible, but that deprived us of the sheltered cruising waters of the popular yachting centres. It kept us independent of other people too, and clubs. In the open sea we learnt by our own mistakes, or rather Richard did. I seemed to to find lots of reasons why I couldn't get away. When I did we made tedious long trips across to the Isle of Wight. I discovered that I was prone to sea sickness. Kerry was not though, and loved the sailing; she does now, end has been a help and encouragement to her father from the beginning. The second year we made a two week cruise in the Solent, with the two children and our big boxer dog. It was a good example of what we should expect, miserable weather, delays, slow lumpy sailing, damp in everything, sea sickness, squalid cramped conditions. There wasn't a lot I enjoyed. it was good experience though, especially for my husband, as we had no engine to help.There remained eighteen months of Air Force time.

We began looking at secondhand boats but the writings of Dr. David Lewis who sailed the world with his wife and two children led us into thinking that the type of craft he had used, a catamaran, would suit us best. Finding little on the market we applied for details of various new designs to see just what such boats were like. An offer came of demonstration sail. Knowing that it was quite impossible for us to ever buy a new boat, let alone such a thoroughbred as the Oceanic, we went anyway. I was delighted. There was more room than I had seen on single null boats twice as long; a huge cockpit where I felt children could play in safety, a wide foredeck that would let me be sure that Richard was safe when sail handling in rough weather. Inside there were two cabins, with double bunks, dressing table and wardrobes, a cosy dinette, a proper toilet compartment with hand basin and elbow room, a convenient galley with a view out. Everywhere there was room to stand upright, the furnishing was smart and cleanable. The designer himself called it a "trailer with sails". Yes, I thought, a woman could make a home on such a boat. I said so, not choosing the words too well. I said "If I could have one of these, I would be quite happy to go". Bill O'Brien, designer, builder and salesman gave more details. A change over in production methods from wood to glass fibre would allow him to sell the early ones at a discount. Richard had prejudice against glassfibre but he too was very impressed. It did not take much calculation to show that we could not have such an expensive boat and hold to our intention of keeping the house to go back to. There was no doubt now of Richard's firmness of purpose, he wasn't going to dig himself to a rut. Once free of the Air Force he was going travelling, and in a boat. I didn't want him to go alone. I didn't want to be too uncomfortable either, in constant fear for the children's safety. Very reluctantly I agreed that I would give up my house. It was put up for sale and we ordered a new Oceanic. Two days later Richard was notified that his gratuity on release would be a thousand pounds less than we expected. Other securities would have to be sacrificed. Again I acquiesed.

He would be free in March, the boat was to launched in May, leaving time for a trial cruise before we sailed finally in August. A sensible schedule it seemed. But for the Hopes things have a habit of going wrong. I was ill, with mumps, and the doctor suspected something else as well. Within days we had to decide; was it still going to be possible to go on our venture, with an additional crew member? I had grave doubts, but we agreed to increase by two more, one to help Richard with the boat, for I was going to be busy with the baby! It was no problem to recruit a nephew, John, ready for a change after completing a five year training in horticulture.The boat building was delayed; no one bought the house. Richard was released and took a temporary job. The summer was hot, my pregnancy gave me trouble; there was just too much to worry about, I fell into apathy. I didn't want to go to sea.

In mid August our third daughter was born, a big disappointment,for we so wanted a son.We soon recognised how fortunate we were.

Finally we sold the house, well below our asking price. It now became clear just how badly the financial side had worked out. Gone was the hope of a straight forward three year cruise; if we were to circle the world we would have to do so in stages, stopping to work, where and at what we knew not, unless able to earn by writing of our travels. Life was beginning to be very insecure. In a few short weeks my home was gone, the furniture sold, treasures packed and stored; we moved to a holiday trailer, the boat still unfinished. I saw the new folk move in to my house and immediately start on all the improvements we had been unable to afford out of income but could with the gratuity now spent on the boat. I thought, not a little bitterly, that they could do so because we had had to sell at a low price in desperation.

Samantha, the new arrival, took a lot of attention though,and I had plenty to occupy me, finalizing lists of provisions, clothing, household equipment, as well as making curtains and cushions.

At last at the end of October, we moved aboard our new home. It was smaller than I remembered, and now we had three children and another adult. Autumn coolness rendered every interior surface wet with condensation; I hated it but was proud of it too, it looked very smart, strong and efficient. Sailing trials were delayed until minor jobs were complete, then the engine would not behave. I knew about Richard and engines, they just don't get along. I remembered the first time he went to sea, and wished we had the two diesels that the design called for, but cost and the need of stowage space and additional water tanks had limited us to a diminutive gasoline engine, a fact we had many a cause to regret.

Layout of the 30 foot Oceanic designed by Bill O'Brien

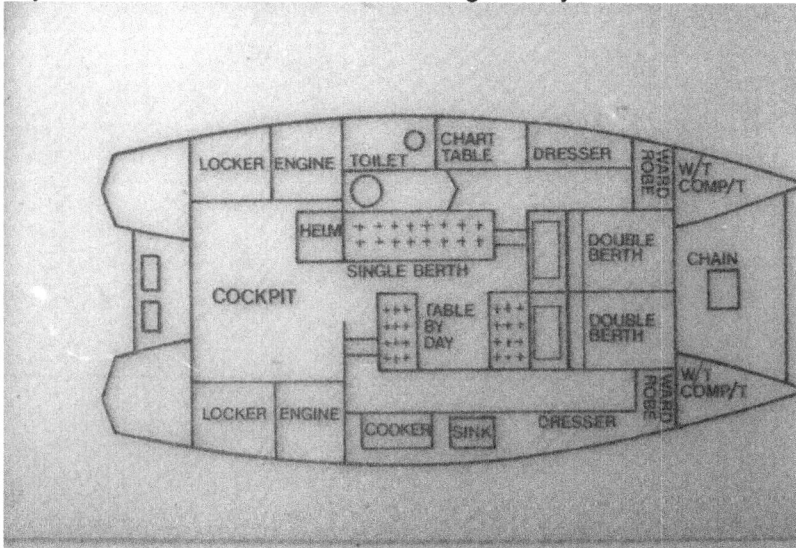

Aboard for the first time.

It was a rush to get away before winter. With the help of friends we sailed from the yard at Southampton to Chichester Marina, to load with our belongings and three months food supply. Family and friends gathered on a sunny November afternoon for a ceremony aboard. Samantha was christened and the boat was blessed.

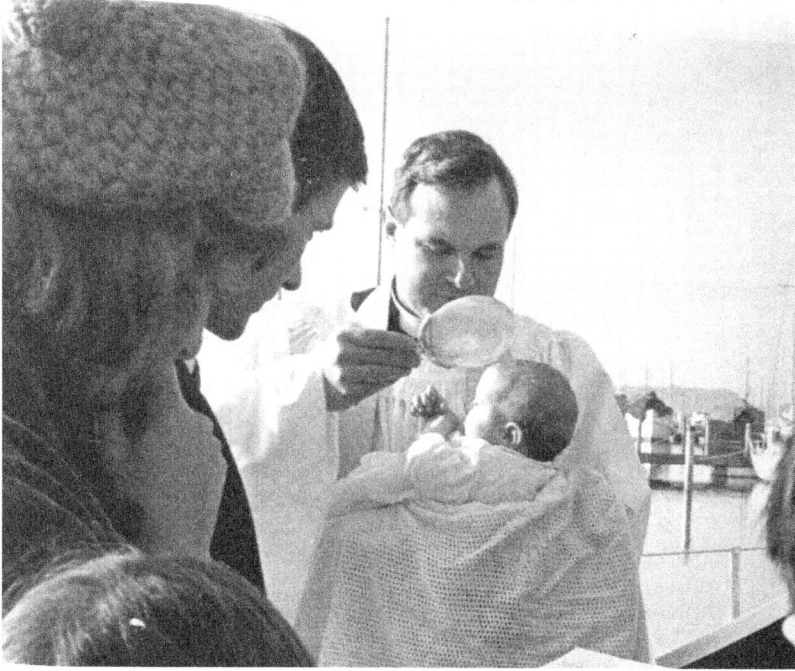

"Motley One" was truly the family home and we felt quite sure that she would carry us all safely wherever we wanted to go. Some of the guests were not so sure, but I was pleased that my parents did not try to dissuade us. I was far from keen but it was what Richard had dreamt of for years and I was ready to give it a try for his sake. He was sure in his own mind that he was not doing it solely for his own satisfaction, feeling that he was making a start on a new life that would give us all adventure, education and a wider outlook.

December lst saw us on our way. From the Marina we sailed around to Selsey Bill, where we had lived for the six years, to take our departure.

Friends had gathered on the beach to wave, car headlights flashed and the coastguard tower emulated a lighthouse. There was a lump in my throat as we sailed away into the misty dusk, anchoring that first night off the end of the pier in Sandown Bay, Isle of Wight. Our crossing to France next day was the first occasion we had ever sailed out of sight of land. The intention was to coast cruise for a few days, out of the way of the busy Channel shipping lanes, learning to handle the boat and settling to life aboard. That went well and I found I could organize housekeeping around my bouts of sea sickness to ensure baby was cared for and the family fed. Kerry helped and stayed fit, Melanie was sick for several days. Richard and John learnt to cope with sails and navigation. The winter gales had set in when we crossed the Bay of Biscay. Well warned of the danger from shipping by the tragedy of a boat like ours, that we saw set off for Japan; and which was run down by a tanker the first night in the Channel, we were being particularly watchful. One night though, hove to in a raging northerly gale we nearly suffered the same fate. A ship turned back after passing us, as if to check on our well being, and must have lost sight of us, for it grazed by, only feet away. Sea sickness, gales, ships and the all pervading wetness were not winning me to the life of a sea rover. Spain was wet and windy. Madeira, reached after a passage so prolonged first by calms then by gale force headwinds, that I began to doubt my husband's navigation, was delightful. Until we left. We were almost driven ashore again by the sudden onset of our most severe storm. It was the end of January by the time we reached the long promised sunshine and warmth. Generally the boat suited us, I would never have lasted in a keel craft, cramped, heeling over and rolling but we had had trouble with leaks. Food and clothing was spoilt, and most upsetting, some of the children's limited and treasured toys, books and games. We had found that the boat was slow and could not easily gain ground against the wind. At Las Palmas in the Canary Islands we restocked with provisions, particularly fresh fruit and vegetables and prepared for the crossing of the Atlantic. The balmy weather did much to convince me that, as Richard said, the worst was behind us. There would be no more storms or headwinds, but there was an awful lot of water before the West Indies. We were all healthy but we carried no radio and would be well away from shipping lanes. I worried, and needed every day of our four week halt to steel myself to going; but though not as stubborn as my husband, I do not think that I could have given up then. The Atlantic was a challenge and romantic notions of the Caribbean a spur. The trade winds were not as helpful as they should have been and it took five weeks to reach Antigua.

Relaxed in the cockpit in mid Atlantic.

I was feeling boredom and impatience toward the end of the passage, but had no fear. Our now well practiced routine of morning and afternoon lessons for Kerry and Melanie kept them and us occupied. Samantha grew, and learnt to crawl in the cockpit and swing from the boom in her bouncer. Soon after our arrival in Antigua, our crew, nephew John, returned to England, to the gardening he decided was preferable to the sea. Without him we would not have got that far, I had been fully occupied with children and housewifery, and still knew nothing of handling the boat. I had never had to do steering watches even, as "Motley One" steered herself quite easily. There being no prospect of employment ashore in the islands and with money getting short we decided to stay in Antigua to earn enough for the next stage by using our boat for day charter work. It was a faint hope at first, for we could not imagine people paying to sail with us, knowing we had three children aboard. We were fortunate on finding a popular middle priced hotel which stayed open, it being by then the 'off' season, and were soon established, anchored in its private bay, offering afternoon cocktail cruises to holiday guests. Our main stay for several months was the custom of the BOAC airline crews who spent rest periods at the hotel. It was good to have company from home but it encouraged the home sickness which had begun to take hold of me. Seeing the charm of the perfectly out-fitted stewardesses emphasized to me how unfeminine continuous life afloat was making me. We were just getting into our stride when Richard was badly burned in a fuel explosion. At anchor off the hotel was better than mid Atlantic though; while he fought the fire I rowed ashore with the children. There was no structural damage so we stayed aboard during the three weeks Richard was in hospital, greatly helped by new friends but with anxious times when the wind blew hard on shore as the engine was out of action. I was grateful for assistance to move to a safer anchorage when a hurricane headed our way. Soon we were active again, earning a few dollars but not busy enough to do more than feed us. It was obvious we would have to remain through the next holiday season. The weather was beautiful, the setting all one expects of the

Caribbean but I was far from content. Our boat which had seemed so large became too small, the confined quarters fraying our nerves. Money was short, prices too high, and the future was very uncertain. I longed for a respite, a holiday trip back to England. The children too were missing their old friends; they had the beach and the sea but rarely any companions of their own age. Lessons took four hours each morning and became a trial with Samantha requiring so much attention. One of us had to spend time ashore, doing the public relations work to find customers. Not till noon each day did I know whether I was going to have guests in my home for the afternoon. The "season" was a long time coming; we had another near disaster. Returning after dark we ran onto a coral reef. After twenty hours of tension and hard work Richard and I dragged our home off the rocks scarred and minus the rudders but not holed. Again friends came to our aid. "Motley" was hauled up the beach and repaired. Three weeks later we were back on station at the hotel, but the episode left us both mentally exhausted. If there had been any alternative we would not have continued then. Our guests of course, all marvelled at our having voyaged from England, and enquired about future plans. The answer stayed the same, that we had set out to sail round the world and were staying in the West Indies just long enough to scrape together finance for the next stage. Early on I felt a fraud, saying that, for it seemed unlikely that we would ever have enough to be able to move on, and I really did not want to go any further anyway. From the Caribbean it was possible to turn and sail back to England, I knew that if we went through Panama we would be committed to continuing westward. Richard would not hear of planning to return to England so I began to answer that perhaps we would decide to settle in New Zealand or Australia. Before long I felt we would have to go on, to avoid disappointing so many nice people who sailed with us. That was what we liked about our charter work, meeting so many wonderful people. Mostly Canadians and Americans with a few English, their praise of our efforts, envious comparisons with more routine, secure lives, boosted my morale. The many teachers we had aboard reassured me that my untrained teaching was not putting Kerry and Melanie behind in scholastic development. We made many many friends and felt that just for that all our struggles had been worthwhile.

So it was that by May I970 we had completed a whole year in Antigua. The 'season' disappointing financially, for all facets of the holiday business, was over. We had worked hard and needed a change. It was to be onward, with fingers crossed. There was no extra crew and I would need to help a lot on with watches as well as cope with the children but we wanted to try keeping it a strictly family affair. I hoped that the sense of humour that had buoyed me up so far would carry me through to a new home in New Zealand.

Journal of the Voyage of 'Motley One'

by Sally Hope.

From Vigo, Spain

. I sit writing aboard our catamaran 'Motley One' which is surging to and fro in the yacht basin of the Real Club Nautico, Vigo, pushed about by gale force gusts of wind and lashed by torrential rain. There has been only one fine day since we arrived a week ago, on January 6th. It's been the same sort of story ever since we left England and the poor weather has put us well behind schedule. Our official and publicised departure was from Chichester Yacht Basin but for us the real moment of truth came two hours later as we sailed past Selsey. Friends were flashing car headlights at us from all around the Bill, the coastguard tower imitated a lighthouse and, as we edged inshore a group gathered on the beach to wave farewell. We had enjoyed living at Selsey for six years and I felt the wrench from my life there, our friends and family far more than any fear of danger or discomfort. I had a big lump in my throat as we turned our stern to the familiar beach and sailed away in the gathering dusk, to stop overnight anchored off the end of the pier in Sandown Bay, Isle of Wight. Setting off so late in the year we should have been hurrying south before the onset of winter weather but we were delaying still further by crossing first to France. The idea was to break the crew in gently with short coastal passages, it being fairly certain that Melanie and I at least would be seasick, and also we would make our way along the Channel clear of the busy shipping lanes. The risk of collision was very clear to us as people we knew had been run down by a ship on their first night out after setting sail a few weeks before us in a similar boat. We did keep clear of the shipping and the crew settled in well during the leisurely progress along the coast but only my Dramamine pills kept the sickness at bay. Melanie gradually got over it and the rest of the crew seemed immune. Five days at Cherbourg, delayed by fog gave us a welcome rest after the hectic weeks of preparation but from there to Morlaix took six days more and I began to wish we had gone straight off on the long passage to Spain. The weather delays were building up and winter had come. The prospect of crossing the Bay of Biscay was even more dismaying. We decided to curtail our coasting and clear from Morlaix for Vigo but it was a long while before the weather would let us.It was December 16th when we left Morlaix with hopes of being in Spain for Christmas but there were warnings of gales in Sole and Biscay so we took a mooring offered by an oyster fisherman at the village of Dourduff-en Mer. On the 20th we made a try but after three hours, having encountered a big swell and rising gale turned back and returned to the mooring. After our roughest ride to date it was good to sit solidly on the mud at low water. I was determined that the girls should have some of the delights of a traditional Christmas despite our situation. I acquired a small tree and John found some lovely holly in a wood on shore. With saved up sweet papers, coloured sticky paper, cotton wool and a variety of bits and pieces I had Kerry and Melanie improvising some most effective decorations. John proved very inventive in this line too. It may seem strange to write of tree and holly decorations in a small yacht but the saloon of 'Motley One' is as spacious as the living room of a large caravan. The bunks are in two separate cabins.   To be ready to sail at the first prospect of good weather we celebrated our Christmas Day on the 24th. The stockings were not as full as perhaps they might have been back home in England but the delight they gave was just as great. Melanie giggled heartily at the sight of nuts in Samantha's tiny sock, for it wasn't till later that day we noticed she had in fact cut her first two teeth, giving the other girls good reason to repeatedly sing 'All I want for Christmas ....'. Crackers and sweets on the tree and a big dinner followed by delicious home made Christmas pudding made a bit of England isolated out there on the mud. Melanie did comment that she didn't receive as many presents as last year but we explained that Father Christmas didn't make personal deliveries to yachts as there were no chimneys but his tiny helpers delivered and they couldn't carry very much. Richard had to go into Morlaix to buy replacements for the fresh provisions we had consumed during our long wait. When he returned he was given a lovely Yule log cake by a woman in the village 'pour les girls'. On the 26th the weather seemed set fair at last so the men made haste to replenish our water stocks. The girls went ashore too, returning with beautifully wrapped parcels for themselves and us from an elderly lady we had spoken with only briefly. People are so kind. It was good to get away under full sail in the sunshine before a light southerly breeze. Not until late in the day when we met the swell left by a week of gales did I make my sacrifice to Neptune. We passed outside Ushant well clear of most shipping but the men kept constant vigilance with Aldis lamp and white flares to hand. Even then I didn't sleep relaxed at night but the children have never been any trouble. The bigger ones sleep through almost anything but Samantha does complain at the noise of rough water. Richard and John do alternate two hour watches, sleeping in between on the single berth in the saloon, keeping most of their clothes on ready to give a hand on deck. The wind rose steadily next day raising a heavy swell and rushing icy rain showers down from the north. By midnight it was so rough that we hove to and prepared to spend thenight keeping careful watch as we were still well in the 'iron road ',the shipping lane that runs south from Ushant. It was about 5 a.m. when we had our big fright. Richard was on watch when a ship appeared from the north. We were not moving appreciably but with navigation lights on he watched. She crossed about a mile ahead but then turned back towards us as if to investigate whether we were faring alright in the gale. Richard illuminated the sails with the bright Aldis lamp and she came up well clear on our starboard bow. Richard again lit up the sails with a green to show that we were a sailing craft and our heading, then direct at the ship to signify we were safe. Suddenly she turned toward us and came right across our bows. I heard a shout of 'She's coming right at us' and looked up from feeding Samantha to see lights towering above us. In an agonising interval I heard Richard swearing then a cry of 'Hang on'. I had baby beside me on the bunk and flung myself over her. Next moment there was a tremendous crash on the port side. I thought the ship had hit us. We were thrown sideways hard and from all over the boat came the noise of things falling. From the shelves above our bunk every book was flung down on me but none hit Samantha. Richard came in to say we were OK though the stern wave had hit us hard. He was very shaken: apparently he could have touched the ships side with the boat hook and only the small turn he had managed to make, swinging the wheel from hard port to hard starboard had taken us from under her bows. He had had the presence of mind to flash a green at the retreating stern of the unknown vessel, not wanting a worried helmsman to come back for a second look. Melanie had only been woken by the crash but poor Kerry hearing the earlier shouting had woken to face the monstrous bows slicing toward her and was very frightened. Miraculously nothing was broken but there was an awful mess on the floor. Perhaps the jolt to the boat seemed much worse at the time because we had not experienced its like before but later in gales we received the same sort of blow repeatedly. The jolt to ourselves though was considerable and nights have been very tense ever since. Next day it was still force 8 but we edged westward under low sail trying to clear the shipping lanes before lying with no sail set for the night. The next two days were better, and we made good progress but on the 31st it began to blow hard again, from the east. In a force 9 wind we lay a hull again, beam on to wind and sea with foaming crests of thirty foot waves breaking frequently against the side, throwing water right over the boat with a fearful noise. An almost full moon in a cloudless sky made the wild scene more awe inspiring than frightening. I've not experienced a force 9 gale in a single hull boat of only thirty foot length but I don't think it can be anywhere near as comfortable as aboard our catamaran. We are on almost an even keel nearly all the time and below life goes on quite normally, the rise and fall of the swell being unnoticeable. In fact it's more difficult to move around when we are sailing with a moderate breeze. The men very much appreciate the warmth and space of the saloon when they come in from the cockpit. A paraffin pressure lamp kept going night and day gives light and warmth. Even in the roughest weather I have prepared normal meals without difficulty. The gas cooker is not gimballed but nothing gets spilt. The hardest thing I find to do is pour milk into the narrow neck of the baby's bottle. When bad weather keeps them below Kerry and Melanie have plenty to keep them busy. I try to guide them with daily lessons and they take it in turns to help with baby or in the galley.

On January I st it was still blowing hard but Richard hoisted the tiny staysail to give us enough way to steer at a slight angle to the swell and reduce the thumping we took. 'Motley One' inched slowly on her way, steering herself while the crew kept warm and dry inside though maintaining a cautious lookout. That's another great advantage of the boat, all round visibility from inside. By morning of the 2nd the wind had fallen very light; three days of glorious weather ensued though with long periods of frustrating calm. The sky remained absolutely cloudless, we had the sun by day and a full moon at night. The children fished with lines and net, Samantha sunbathed on deck and Richard rowed off in the dinghy to photograph us, swilling around in flat calm with full sail set. A school of dolphins paid us a visit, delighting the girls. In very light airs we closed the coast of Spain on the 5th not sighting anything till we were within four miles because of thick haze. We had twenty miles to run southward to Vigo, where we entered next day after a night which went from dead calm to raging gale with heavy rain and hail which we later learnt broke a fine spell that had run from December 22nd.

If the weather clears soon we'll have a day or two cruising in the lovely Ria de Vigo before sailing for Madeira, as yet we've seen little except the town.

MOTLEY ONE

'Motley One' Journal

by Sally Hope.

From Las Palmas

Our stay in Madeira lasted just a week. Anchored close to the pier in Funchal harbour, 'Motley One' was used as a traffic island by the ferry boats which operate from it, carrying passengers between the town and the many cruise liners which call. The constant activity gave the children plenty of interest and they were soon friendly with the ferrymen while the passengers delighted in the sight of Samantha dangling happily from the boom on her bouncer. Ashore the girls were fascinated by the gay sledges drawn by oxen and countless bazaars crammed with tourist impedimenta. The children in turn attracted a lot of interest particularly Samantha who I took around in her two wheeled chair, smiling cheekily at everyone. The weather was not as nice as we had expected and we were told that the winter was proving severe by Madeiran standards but we did find a need for summer clothes at last. The rain which fell so heavily as we arrived had caused extensive flooding and landslide damage. In such a short stay it was impossible to see much of this delightful island, but Richard did take Kerry and Melanie for a day-long walking expedition up the mountain beyond Funchal. They returned very weary but having spent so long afloat the children did very well to get so far, right up to the woods at cloud level, and back through the banana plantations. I had to stay behind with Samantha, the climb being too steep for me to manage with her, and I had an accumulation of household chores which are much more easily dealt with when the rest of the crew are ashore. The French aircraft carrier 'Clemenceau' called on a courtesy visit and her shore boats were very busy around us. One sailor took an interest in 'Motley' and came aboard for a look. In return he invited Kerry and I to visit his 'sheep', an occasion we thoroughly enjoyed, having a guided tour, seeing a lot denied to the invasion of the local public. Kerry was most embarrassed, earning her 'lucky pom-pom' from the French sailors hat by giving him a kiss.
We also met a French couple aboard another yacht bound for the West Indies. Andre Hougron sailed 'Anore' single handed from Le Croisic direct to Madeira. His wife Bernadette flew out to join him for the remainder of the

voyage.

On Sunday 16th we departed for the Canary Islands, having to motor clear in flat calm. By nightfall though there was too much wind. A fierce southerly gale sprang up and we were all but driven ashore, needing the engines aid to beat clear. Later the wind turned westerly so that on Monday we sought shelter in the lee of the rugged Ilhas Desertas. With no sail set we rode out a Force 10 gale using a heavy warp to slow our drift. Not until Wednesday morning could we set small sails and begin to work our way south-ward. As always seems our fortune the wind remained against us. Until Sunday morning we beat against it, making a very wearying passage, then again we had our 'arrival weather', drizzle and calm. Only this time the calm was too complete and the engine wouldn't start, so we didn't arrive. The next day was better, a faint breeze and warm sun. Gran Canaria was in sight and slowly we crept in to anchor amidst the bustle and filth of the big harbour of Las Palmas. Soon we met the Hughes family of Bournemouth, about to set off across the Atlantic in their trimaran 'Warm Winds'. Having been here for three months they were able to help us a great deal with directions on finding supplies and services. It seems that our story of constant contrary winds and fierce gales is far from unusual. Here too we have met a Dane, Freda Petersen, who has now set sail for the West Indies alone, in a tiny 18'6" British built Alacrity. He expects to take anything up to 60 days so that if, as we hope, our stay lasts only two weeks, we may pass him. Las Palmas of course is a thriving tourist and holiday resort of cosmopolitan character. The food shops carry enormous stocks of a fantastic variety of foods from all countries, with prices just a little higher than at home. Provisioning the boat for the Atlantic crossing, allowing two months at sea, is going to be a real headache.The men are very busy carrying out minor repairs and making improvements. We are anchored close to a sandy beach where the children love to play, and bathe when the oil which usually pervades the harbour clears away. The yacht club which has made us welcome gives an easy access to the shore. One diversion has been the loss of one anchor when its warp cut through on the rocks. Richard eventually found and recovered it by diving. A major disappointment has been the loss of our mail. Nearly all of what we know has been sent has failed to arrive. We are now really enjoying the sunshine we've sought after, but with so much to do we find little time to relax in it, though we can work outside in swimming costumes. Already we have been here a week. Most of the jobs are done. We wait for our mail, some new parts for the toilet, which hasn't worked for weeks, and then we'll complete our provisioning with fresh vegetables and fruit. Although not enchanted at the prospect of six or seven weeks confined to a small boat amidst thousands of miles of empty Atlantic, I dread it less now that I can believe more easily in the promise of good weather. I'm impatient to make a start, and hoping for a fast passage to get it over with. I hope to be able to write next time of dreamy days of carefree trade wind sailing, flying fish lying on deck for breakfast and dorados swimming alongside asking to be caught for lunch.

MOTLEY ONE

'Fwee Four Fizzle'

by Sally Hope

How's the course?' calls my husband, Richard. There's a hand compass on the table near me, kept there so that we can keep an eye on the way we are going as our mobile home trundles along with no one at the helm. My youngest daughter, Samantha (2years) hearing, peers at it, 'Fwee Four Fizzle' she declares. Not that she can read the compass yet but we've been checking the course aloud for some time. I glance to confirm it. Richard is busy with Kerry (12) and Melanie (7) giving them Biology interest as he dissects a large Dorado caught on a trailing line, baited with one of the small flying fish often found on deck in the morning. Dorados are such beautiful coloured fish it makes me sad to see them die. They flash silver and blue with golden tails in the water. Once aboard they first go golden all over then try to hide by assuming the bright blue of the fibreglass deck, fading to silver as they die. We catch 'Old Wives' too, so called because of their tough skins! Small shoals of these join us and swim with us at times for days. These are the only fish I know with eyelids. Richard swears they wink at him. Asking to be caught? Later I will use today's catch to prepare Cebiche, a dish of peppers and raw fish popular with the family since we learned it in Peru. An invitation to visit friends drew us to Peru; we stayed five months. From Panama we had tried to reach the Galapagos Islands before sailing southward to Callao, but at that time of year wind and current were strongly against us: we were compelled to miss out the 'Tortoise Islands and had a prolonged struggle down the coast. So it was at the end of a three month voyage and after two years living aboard we found it especially enjoyable to reach Lima and stay for a month in a house. There were beds that did not rock, hot baths, washing and drying machines and space, space. We all loved the colourful flowers and green lawns, such a contrast to the sea always at our doorstep. The girls had room to play, energetic games and with much missed prams and bicycles. I appreciated the enormous kitchen, many times the size of my tiny galley. The whole of our 30ft Catamaran would fit into the lounge. Samantha was fascinated by the stairs and variety of toilets, all three girls marvelled at the size of

the bedrooms. Aboard 'Motley One' Melanie and
Samantha share one tiny cabin, Kerry has a similar one
and Richard and I sleep in the saloon. A difficult thing to
accustom ourselves to again was the traffic noise and
bustle of people; these and the Spanish language kept us
ill at ease whenever we ventured out. In January the
Peruvian schools closed for three months. With much to do
before setting forth again we settled back aboard the boat,
moored at the Yacht Club at Ancon, a summer resort. The
children, making friends amongst English families there,
had a wonderful time and the same long period free of
lessons. They were learning Spanish though, and
attended Folklore and Gymnastic classes. One lady taught
Kerry French and another took her water skiing. We often
feel that the girls miss much by not having companions
their age; our long stay in Peru made up for a lot. The
highlight of the visit was going with our host, David Stone,
to the ancient Inca city of Cuzco; unfortunately David's
wife, Rosalie, could not accompany us to an altitude of
l2,000ft because she was expecting her third child, but she
looked after Samantha for three days, a playmate for her
own young daughter. The jet flight over the Andes was a
great thrill and from Cuzco we went on the scenic train ride
to Machu Picchu, the 'lost' city of the Incas, incredibly
perched on a mountain top. There can never have been
more appreciative travellers there than we were. How we
loved the green valleys and mountains after months of sea
and desert coast. We had prepared ourselves for this
tourist journey while we made the laborious passage down
from Panama. It's our habit to direct the children's studies
toward the next destination so we learned of the Inca
history, the Geography of Peru and its development.While
at sea we try to maintain a daily programme of lessons,
with weekends free so that for Kerry and Melanie it is as
much like school as we can make it. Richard takes Kerry
for most of her subjects and I have Melanie to coach in
reading and writing, science,while handicrafts and general
interest are dealt with jointly. A favourite is cooking which
produces cakes, biscuits and puddings that we all
enjoy.Before we left England we obtained from the local
school all the books both girls would have used there in the

following two years. We are somewhat behind on that syllabus, but they have learnt other things instead. History and Geography with on the spot illustration, languages, money systems and a wide field of general knowledge.There are distractions from school work too. Going to Peru, constantly near the coast, amongst shipping and often in fog it was necessary for Richard and I to keep watches overnight, instead of letting 'Motley One' sail on her own as we do in the open ocean. That often left us too tired in the daytime to take 'school', then the girls had to amuse themselves, which they are extremely good at doing. A great portion of the excess load that the boat staggers along with is composed of their books, games, dolls (20+) and handwork. A Lego building set gives hours of fun. Visitors call too. Yesterday an enormous mixed shoal of 25ft whales and smaller porpoises found us. They stayed an hour leaping and somersaulting all about, frolicking right between the bows. They like an audience and we do not disappoint them however often they call. Leaving my galley duties to go on deck to watch I remember to close the window. We have had food on the stove spoilt by a deluge from a crash dive alongside. At other times there are whales, turtles, sea snakes or fish, sometimes ships passing close. Now we are making a 'downhill' run, the wind astern, the current favourable from Peru to the 'Enchanted' isles of Galapagos. School is in session regularly and we are trying to catch up after a gap of five months. Samantha is a difficulty now for she wants to participate in whatever the girls do; 'Teacher me Mummy' she demands and at times it becomes almost impossible to get anything done with the others unless Richard or I give her full attention. In December 1968 when we sailed from England the situation was rather different. To help Richard with the boat handling we had our nephew John Matthews (21) and with Samantha only three months old sleeping a lot, I was able, when once over the sickness which beset me for the first four days of each passage, to give much more attention to the education and amusement of the other two. The inclement weather in the early stages beating southward, across Biscay in January to Spain, Madeira and Canary Islands, plus the fact that knowing little of sailing I was no help on deck, made it conducive to remain inside. For the long passage across the Atlantic I had to steel myself, but the children had quite taken to life aboard. The five weeks it took us to reach the West Indies were not frightening though, just rather tedious; the one period of interest when we were becalmed for nearly a week. Then we saw and caught fish, and found a floating bottle with a note in, dropped in the sea exactly one year before. It was a relief to be in warmer, dryer conditions. Samantha learnt to crawl,perfectly safe in the large cockpit. To occupy myself and the girls we knitted toys, crotched, made dolls clothes and models utilising all sorts of scraps, for we save food cartons for drawing and making things, magazines for 'cutting out'. From Antigua John returned home and with just the family as crew we established ourselves with a hotel, anchored in it's private bay, offering afternoon sailing cruises to the holiday guests. Our aim was to earn and save enough to voyage further but it was a slow start in the 'off season'. The situation was idyllic, and we made the most of it. Melanie learned to swim, Kerry became very proficient and Samantha developed wonderful confidence using arm floats. Two near disasters almost put an end to our plans; first we had a fuel fire that put Richard into hospital for several weeks, then we stranded our home on a coral reef, but fortunately got it off again with only the loss of the rudders. In each case we received tremendous assistance from friends we had met on the island, and so it has been wherever we have stopped. It is the people we meet, their interest and generous help and the lasting friendships we make that give us encouragement to continue our journey. During the year we stayed in Antigua we continued with school on board in the mornings. For me it was an exacting time, the boat the focal point of interest for folk on the beach, and I never knew until midday whether I would have my home full of guests for the afternoon. Not that they were strangers, often we knew them quite well having frequently met on the beach before. In this way we made a host of friends, mostly from Canada and the USA. The 'season' eventually proved disappointing financially, but we felt we must try to move on. I had qualms about long passages with no other crew but after a wonderful holiday cruise through the other islands, I agreed we could cope,so we set out westward again via Curacao to Panama.

Now before us is the part of the voyage we have dreamed of for so long, the South Seas, with New Zealand as our goal. If all goes well we'll be there before Christmas, to seek work, stay perhaps a year, then consider whether to continue on around the world. It will take some deciding, for we have found that a life aboard a small yacht with three children is quite a full one.

The End

Sally Hope
Academy Bay
Santa Cruz
Galapagos Islands
          May 1971

MOTLEY ONE

We Saw 'Le Bomb'

by

Richard C Hope

In July and August of 1971, the British catamaran 'Motley One' on route to Tahiti from Peru, visited islands on the fringe of the French nuclear test zone. We knew that there was to be another series of French nuclear tests before we left Peru but the Naval Attache's Office of the French Embassy in Lima was unable to give us details of the areas designated as 'prohibited', though they are, in fact, in International waters. Neither could we gain any information from the Equadorians in the Galapagos Islands or the Chilean Port Captain of Easter Island. Our plan, therefore, was to call at Mangareva, in the Gambier Islands, at the eastern extremity of French Polynesia, which, being over 200 miles from the test site, and inhabited, was obviously outside the danger area but probably within the jurisdiction of the military controllers. On arrival at Pitcairn though, we found that Tom Christian, the Radio Officer, made daily contact with Tahiti during the testing period so he requested routing instructions for us. The reply, under the authority of the Governor of French Polynesia, authorised us to enter at Mangareva. We found the Pitcairn Islanders quite concerned about the testing though not too clear on what they are afraid of. On such a small, remote island the terms pollution and ecology do not have much significance. The Sunday before our arrival the sound of the last test explosion, made over 500 miles away, had been clearly heard, during a quiet interval, by the whole population assembled in church. Marooned on the island by the ship 'Sir Percival' which carried the British scientific and military observers of the tests, were two RAF. Technicians. Their duty was to tend the monitoring instruments set up on a high point of Pitcairn to detect any radio active fall-out. The presence of these technicians perhaps encouraged the islanders suspicions of the French programme, and had them asking what would happen to their peaceful community of 93 people if the instruments did suddenly record a fall of dust. However, it does seem improbable that Pitcairn could be affected because of the intervening distance and prevailing winds and currents. Reluctantly we left the 'Bounty' island and its friendly, hospitable people, and sailed westward with 280 nautical miles to go, to Mangareva. After calms and strong winds from the northwest, we actually got into the lagoon on the eleventh day, but the sudden onset of violent squalls damaged our sails and with the engine useless we were blown away again.We finally re-entered through the southeast passage on the 20'" day after leaving Pitcairn. Numerous manta rays 6 - 8 ft. across, flapped lazily out of our path as we picked our way between shoals to join the buoyed channel in from the north west passage to the anchorage of the village of Rikitea.

The Gambier Islands are a group of volcanic. formation enclosed by a barrier reef of coral, amid a deep lagoon studded with coral patches. The principal island is Mangareva, dominated by Mount Bluff (1,400 ft.) still black when we arrived from a bush fire that had provided us with a guiding beacon on our first approach. The majority of the groups people now live on Mangareva, in and around Rikitea, and now number less than 600, a quarter of what Fathers Laval and Caret of the Pupus Order of Chile found on their arrival in 1834. Six years later there were more than 2,000 Christians, but there had been hundreds of deaths. Father Laval had driven the islanders, unused to heavy labour, too hard in his ambitious projects to construct churches, roads and a convent. The latter nowstands in ruins, but the churches of the lesser islands can still be seen and the twin square towers of Rikitea's monster, built to hold 1,200 people tower above the trees that hide the nestling houses, a monument to Laval, who was recalled to Tahiti in 1871. The sound of an aircraft surprised us, as still engineless, we gingerly crept through the coral strewn passage to the anchorage and we watched in amazement as the airliner swept in to a landing apparently on the water across the northern end of the lagoon. Later we leant that an airstrip had been constructed on the reef by connecting several sandy islets, and the French Navy had established a base there.Very soon the Gendarme, who represents French authority to the Islanders, came out to give us clearance. The cable from Tahiti was sufficient authorisation and we were simply asked to give a day's notice of intended departure. Our proximity to the test area was made clear by the Gendarme's strict warning that we should not eat fish.

Those in the lagoon were poisoned by 'le dust', radio active fallout. The islanders were friendly enough but few spoke French, only Polynesian, so we could not communicate well until we met a family from Tahiti, on holiday with the father, who was stationed on the island in charge of the Travaux Publiques. Madame and the eldest daughter spoke excellent English and the younger children were good companions for our daughters, Kerry (13), Melanie (8), and Samantha (3). The village stretches out along a firm sand and gravel road between the lagoon and rocky hills which carries only the gendarme's jeep, the Public Works truck and excavator, and the island's single car, property of the Catholic priest. This gentlemen, elderly but erect and active, possessed of a grey goatee beard, and usually seen wearing a white pith helmet, keeps a tight rein on his flock. Only one family on the island is Protestant, and they have to maintain their own shop, the other stores being owned by the Father, who denies their use to non-Catholics and, for periods, to those of his 'family' who fail to attend church regularly. As visitors we were admitted to those shops but there was little to be bought. A few essentials are flown in, but the bulk of provisions arrives by sea, and no ships are permitted during the test programme. Many of the menfolk have been given work by the military and around the island we saw evidence of new prosperity: two new restaurants, a litter of beer bottles despoiling the roadside, and new outboard engines for the boats the fishermen can no longer use with profit. The weekly air service which now connects Mangareva with Tahiti gives the people a hope that, when the nuclear test programme is over and work for the men finishes, the group will develope as a tourist resort. We heard rumours that the Club Mediterraneé hopes to buy one of the smaller islands. There was plenty for us to do aboard 'Motley One' repairing the engine and mending sails, so we had no time for exploring around the lagoon. Toward the end of the second week, I moved the boat into a beach so that I could do some repair work under the bows when she grounded at low tide. On the shore close by was a small French unit staffed by one Army Lieutenant and a naval rating. The officer, serving his compulsory one year, unpaid, national service was a newly qualified veterinarian. That had got him the sinecure he enjoyed at Mangareva, and was just about to relinquish at the end of his engagement. Fully qualified as he was, he had the gross task of catching just 4 kilos of a particular type of fish each week, sealing them in polythene and sending them by air to Tahiti. To fill the task he had six boats, the naval rating and a native island boatman, his own mess and civilian catering staff. No wonder research is expensive.

Around 9.30 a.m. on August 8th, we heard the rumble of the scheduled test explosion at Muraroa, 240 nautical miles to the west. It was not loud, like distant thunder, but Mount Duff was in between. Soon after noon, while I was working beneath Motley, applying fibreglass, the church bells began to ring in an agitated fashion. Within minutes, the Gendarme appeared, and ordered us to leave everything and go to the 'Braucas'. We guessed he meant the large building at the far end of the village, which we had taken to be an Army storehouse, but Kerry had heard that it was used as a shelter. Our Army neighbours disappeared very promptly, and as we could not see anyone else we thought we had better hurry. While I endeavoured to clear most of the resin from my hands changed into dry clothes Sally cleared clothing from lines, outside, and stowed away all the fresh food, closed windows and hatches. Taking only a few biscuits and games for the children we hurried ashore and up into the village.

We were far from last. The whole population was on the move struggling up the road, children laden with bundles and younger brethren, adults carrying bedding and food. All available transport was in use, ferrying the old folk, invalids and children. The earthmover rumbled along, its bucket loaded with suitcases, bundles wrapped in gay linen prints and sometimes small boys. For our benefit there were a few caustic comments about the 'bloody French' and 'le Bomb'.

Despite the general air of gaiety the islanders infuse into almost everything they do it was plain that they did resent the interference with their normal peaceful life. Our three girls, sent on ahead, were waiting in the assembling crowd, at the building, about a mile from the boat . It began to rain then and there was a scramble to shelter beneath the trees and doorways while we waited for everyone to collect and for somebody to arrive with the key. Army officers were there with encouraging rumours that it was only an exercise to last two or three hours, an excuse to butter up the local population by paying them for a missed days work even though it was a Sunday. Eventually the gendarme and the mayor began checking people into the shelter, family by family, supervised by the Army. The Hopes were almost the last, and we walked through two sections of the hangar like building to find ourselves beds near our Tahitian friends. Electric lights were on for the Braucas has no windows and it was cool from the humming air conditioning. Soon pumps began to throb, continually spraying water over the roof to wash away any radio active cloud that might fall, the water was channelled straight back to the lagoon! Each of the four accommodation rooms are about 100 feet square; between there are blocks of offices for the military, storerooms, kitchens and much to our girls' disgust, French style communal toilets. For two hours or so there was little to do. Rumours were rife, but there was no official pronouncement. The children ran nosily wild, adults tried to be patient, and make themselves comfortable on the only furnishings, camp beds and wooden stools. Groups gathered around guitar strummers to sing,the lilting polynesian songs, oblivious of the dingy surroundings and the grim reason for their incarceration.At 5 p.m. the men were called out to collect rations for their families but when I joined the queue outside the storeroom I was admitted the back way to get our issue: two litre bottles of water, two tins each of beef, fish, peaches and fruit juice and two packs of hard tack biscuits. Quite a feast. The kitchens, equipped with spotless stainless steel were immaculate, never having been used, and the Army wanted to keep them that way. Women were allowed use of only one cooker in one kitchen to heat food for children. There was no way to make a hot drink and we were dying for a cup of tea. We had no tin opener, crockery or cutlery with us but were able to borrow, the villagers had been into the Braucas twice before for short periods and were prepared. When it became dark it seemed reasonable to suppose that we were there for the night for it would have been difficult for many people to get home and it was raining hard too. At 7 p.m. the mayor announced that there would be a film show and that we were staying 'till morning. I took my stool along and found a place in the end section where the film was to be shown, a little too early, for there was a Catholic prayer meeting first. The chanting of the rosary prayers in Polynesian seemed musical at first but to my ears, soon sounded monotonously repetitive. Sally, after vainly trying to settle Samantha to sleep, joined the Protestant meeting of about a dozen persons at the other end of the building. Later she crept into watch the film, which was English, dubbed in French, 'Ill Met by Moonlight". After a scanty, cold supper from the rations, Sally and the girls settled to sleep, covered with a large sheet of brightly patterned cloth lent by a dear old lady. The canvas beds had to be carefully checked for centipedes. Many were found, 4 - 6 inches long, able to inflict a nasty, poisonous bite. I wandered restlessly for a time, and will always remember the scenes in those cavernous rooms. Large groups of beds were pushed close together for family unity, all were covered in gay, printed cotton covers, many with varied cushions and with the bright clothing of the people sitting or lying on them, made a brilliant patchwork of colour so much in contrast to the starkness enclosing them. It rained heavily all night, but the pumps still worked nosily and the chill filtered air made sleeping difficult. In desperation I unlaced the canvas from an unused bed and used that as a blanket. When word went around at 7 a.m. that we were free to go it was a relief to tramp out into sunshine just breaking through as the heavy rain clouds cleared away. The ground was sodden, the trees dripping, but the air smelt sweet and fresh and it was good to have the assurance that no dust had been detected on the island. The dispersal of the 500 or so villagers was the reverse of gathering, the vehicle shuttle service and everyone plodding along laden with baggage like returning refugees, but the gaiety was missing, nearly all were tired, and it was Monday morning. As we walked back we noted the pigs, chickens and domestic animals left loose and exposed, and we imagined the loss and disruption that could be caused by any contamination from a nuclear test. Our boat was a little more motley for protective polythene sheeting had blown away and the resin I had applied before being rushed away had set in unsightly runs down the hull. That was all that made me cross. Three days later we set sail for Tahiti. Another test was due, the biggest of the series, but the Gendarme cleared our departure with the military authorities on the understanding that we intended to sail south around the circle, radius120 nautical miles from Muraroa. I would have liked to go up into the Tuamotus but the danger zone has a sector extending north-eastward, the path, out into empty ocean, of the bulk of the fallout. The winds were not helpful and we did not keep to the schedule I had outlined to the Gendarme but we were well outside the restricted area. During the afternoon of August 13th the ship 'Brambleleaf 'of London passed close, a Naval Auxiliary vessel I thought, and, I wondered if she was connected with the observer effort. We had heard that ships of all nations interested in the test programme, clustered around the area jostling for position. in case any of them were in our path we kept careful watch. Soon after 4 a.m. that night Sally woke me with an urgent voice. An aircraft was making a low pass, bathing us in brilliant light, probably a maritime aircraft of the French navy checking our position. It made a long leg to the south then passed directly over us at a higher level without signalling. That assured me that we were identified and known to be out of danger. It also suggested that the test was imminent. At dawn I took a star fix which confirmed my reckoning, over 150 nautical miles from Muraroa. Later there was an enormous bank of cloud over toward the direction of the test atoll and it seemed unlikely that we would see anything of the explosion. At 9.30 a.m. I decided we had either missed it or that it was again postponed and went to the cabin to sleep. I had barely settled when Melanie called from the cockpit that she had heard the bomb. I looked out and could see the typical mushroom cloud already well developed, the normal cloud there earlier having cleared a little to the east. The rest of us got into the cockpit just in time to hear the full report of the explosion, a sharp crack like a distant field gun. In the next two or three minutes it was followed by several rumbles and small separate reports. The white cloud towered way up, its top spreading out like a double anvil. It was still identifiable when I woke two hours later, by then a large patch of dirty looking layer cloud at the level of cirrus

 I would not say that what we saw was awe inspiring, no more spectacular than the sight of a satellite passing across the sky. We have lived with knowledge of such things for too long. The significance of it though was apparent enough even to our eight year old. The direct danger to people is minimal and, presumably, other inhabited islands near the test area have Braucas shelters like Mangareva but their environment is endangered and the radioactive dust does fall into the sea to affect its life and be carried to distant parts.

   Pacific countries are vocal in their protests against this pollution but so far Governments make only formal motions of disapproval. The only action is that a couple of yachts set sail from New Zealand to try to enter the test area. I cannot believe they will be allowed anywhere near Muraroa.

MOTLEY ONE

The Family on arrival in Whangerei, New Zealand

What Happened Later?

After the visit to Mangareva and the sighting of the French test, of what turned out to be their first Hydrogen Bomb, Motley reached Papeete, Tahiti, where a long stay of seven weeks, for a variety of reasons, meant that the onward voyage to New Zealand had to be hurried. Instead of following the usual yachting route, to the Cook Island, there was a short visit to what is often called the worlds most remote island, Palmerston Atoll and a meeting with the descendants of William Marsters, then to Niue a small island administrated by New Zealand, rarely a port of call for sailing boats, then on to Vavau before the final last leg to Whangerei in the North Island of New Zealand, arriving just before Christmas. Three years having been spent getting there, the time originally allowed for the whole circum-navigation, it was time to put the childrens education first. The Immigration Authority allowed entry as immigrants and a new life started. Kerry was just in time to start at the secondary school, there being a three tiered system, and Melanie went to Primary. Both fitted in well with their basic skills levels equating with their age group. Samantha was by then three years old.

Unable to find suitable jobs we elected to start a business, with encouragement and finance of a couple met in Tahiti who had also made the voyage. Our venture was a basic Launderette, because there wasn't one and visiting yachties had nowhere to get their laundry done. After a while I started work as a builders labourer, working for another yachtie met in Tahiti. I soon suffered a back injury, lifting heavy timbers. New friends sent me to see a Chiropractor, a sort of practitioner that I had not heard of before. He not only fixed the immediate problem but on X-rays showed that I had become prone to such because of damage done when I was in the helicopter crash while in the RAF. The knowledge and skill demonstrated set me thinking that I would like to join the profession, which of course meant a long formal training. I applied to a fairly new College in Bournemouth, England, and was soon accepted , as a mature student. All I had to do was get there. Unable to sell the boat we had no capital to finance a return to the UK. Still wishing to complete what I had set out to do, complete a circumnavigation, I decided the way to get back was to sail. Sally remaining in New Zealand, earning with our small business and with the children settled in school, I would go alone, single handed, and not having the time or resources to stop on the way, I would do the voyage non-stop.

I did, but the account of that voyage will be told elsewhere.

Suffice to say I made it back, taking seven months. Sally and the girls then flew back. I sold Motley and went to College for four years. After graduation I set up in practice on the Isle of Wight, and in time got another boat, another catamaran!

MOTLEY ONE

A final article is another written in New Zealand, describing the voyage of Motley One for the readers of a yachting magazine, making the point that Catamarans Can Cope.Motley One, pictured above shortly after launching at Southampton in 1968 is a 30 foot Oceanic class catamaran now berthed in Town Basin, Whangerei. She was sailed halfway round the world by the Hope family RIchard and Sally, with daughters Kerry (now13), Melanie(8)and Samantha (3),who was only three months old at the beginning of the three year voyage.
 Richard, who is an agent for Bill O'Brien Catamarans, now tells about the characteristics of this type of floating family home, asserting that

CATAMARANS CAN COPE

CATAMARANS CAN COPE

Motley One, pictured above shortly after launching at Southampton in 1968 is a 30 foot Oceanic class catamaran now berthed in Town Basin, Whangerei. She was sailed halfway round the world by the Hope family RIchard and Sally, with daughters Kerry (now13), Melanie(8)and Samantha (3),who was only three months old at the beginning of the three year voyage.

Richard, who is an agent for Bill O'Brien Catamarans, now tells about the characteristics of this type of floating family home, asserting that

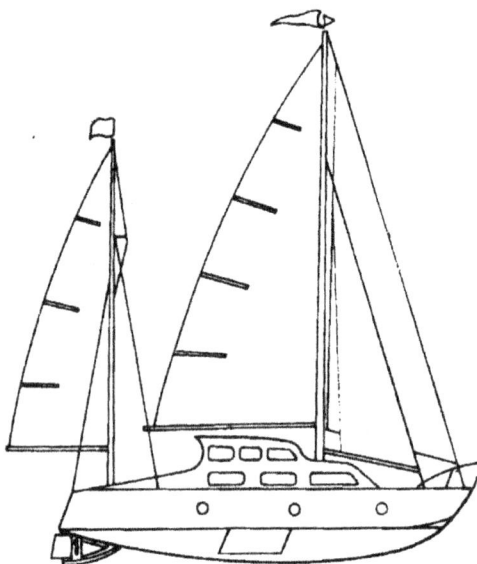

Motley One, designed by Bill O'Brien. 30ft overall length, 14ft 4in beam, 2ft draught and displacing 3.7 tons. Moulded in fibreglass and ketch rigged with 480sq ft of working sail

THE OCEANIC class has been in production since 1966 and 60 boats have been built. A motor sailer concept, the design was a development of the Bobcat, which, still being produced, must be the most numerous type of cruising catamaran in the world. The initials B.O.B., of course, come from the name of the designer, Bill O'Brien, who was one of the first successful catamaran designers in Britain. Rapid growth in the Oceanic's popularity in the '60s drew to sailing a lot of maturer men who had little or no experience. Wives and children wanted to accompany them, but many could not put up with the inconvenience, confinement and discomfort of small monohulls.

There was an open market for the cruising catamaran for the stability and space it offered. It is true that trimarans, too, grew in popularity for the same reasons but in small versions, 35 foot and less, they cannot offer the internal accommodation that a catamaran of the same size provides. Early development of multihulls had emphasised their speed potential and generally, the tendency was towards designs to exploit that. Accommodation, cruising equipment and auxiliary power were restricted by the requirement for lightness. Such light, unballasted boats, with large areas of sail to give speed, were fine in good conditions in the hands of expert crews, but there was an inherent danger of capsize. Indeed, one 30-footer being tested by a continental yachting magazine did turn completely upside down. The result was a rash of cruising catamarans sporting masthead buoyancy chambers, which did little to encourage doubting wives and beginners in sail. Bill O'Brien followed a different line. His aim was to take advantage of the stability and spaciousness of the catamaran to provide a comfortable cruising home, with caravan-like accommodation, to encourage full family participation in sailing. Also,he wanted to be sure that he could sell his designs to the most inexperienced, confident that they could sail them without danger of capsize or damage from heavy weather. Speed was a lesser consideration. The Oceanic was developed for people who wanted, for UK coastal and continental cruising, a little more length, his original Bobcat was 26ft, top quality interior furnishing and minimal maintenance, with the added convenience of adequate inboard power units. For optimum use of overall length a solid foredeck is desirable, but this makes windward sailing a pounding performance. The motor-sailer configuration gets around this problem for inboard diesels obviate the necessity for beating to windward under sail, a factor which is important to the majority of weekend yachtsmen, who often have to operate from congested harbours or mooring miles from open water, yet require assurance of timely return on Sunday evening.

Some buyers plumped for marinised car engines, but at 29hp plus each they provided more power per pair than necessary. Bill standardised on the Volvo Penta MDII diesel. Requiring additional stowage space and water-carrying capacity, we decided to have only one engine in Motley One and in the end costs decreed the choice of a Smart Turner 10hp two-stroke petrol motor. When all is in good order this gives 4+ knots on still water, which rather puts the boat out of the motor-sailer class and we have had to regard Motley One strictly as a sailing machine which has been a little unkind, considering the loads we've made her carry. The standard layout provided seven berths, in two double cabins, a double dinette berth and a single in the saloon. Our only modification was to divide the berth in one cabin with a centreboard, to keep the two older girls apart. Sally and I had the other cabin and there was room on the side dressing table to sleep the baby, first in a carrycot and later in a mini berth guarded with rail and net. For the initial part of the voyage, to help me with the boat while Sally attended to the baby, housekeeping and lessons, we had a crew, my nephew, John, who took the saloon berth. We did add extra shelves but the interior layout gives ample stowage, with first class joinery in sealed teak and laminates and foam backed vynide lining. In place of the usual second engine and its fuel tank we fitted two additional water tanks, giving a total capacity of 104 gallons. The fuel tanks hold 32 gallons.

For stability the Oceanic has a beam of more than 14 feet, a low sail plan (480sq ft working) on a ketch rig, with the weight of interior furnishings, water and fuel tanks and two engines low in the hulls.

The hulls themselves are hard chined, with a maximum beam of 5ft. No centreboards are fitted, so the draught is only 2ft. Small bilge keels are fitted to the inboard sides of each hull to reduce sideways slide on wave faces when sailing beam-on to big seas. Initial production was in marine ply with GRP sheathing, but No. 15 onward have been constructed completely in fibreglass, on moulds. The first six boats had a low coach roof over the centre section, with only sitting headroom under it, but afterwards this was raised, converting the bridge area to a sizeable saloon with more than 6ft headroom. From its inception the Oceanic has been also offered in a straight motor cruiser version, but as the power enthusiast that went on the same demonstration sail as I did saw so easily, the sails are not difficult to handle, all halyards and sheets being led to the cockpit, and they do provide adequate performance without the noise, so all buyers have said, as he did, "I'll have some of them, too! Externally, particularly with the fibreglass craft, there is little requiring maintenance, all stainless rigging, bronze and brass fittings and tufnol winches. Windows are safety glass in anodised aluminium frames. Wood trim is teak and, for appearance and foot kindliness, the decks are laid teak strip, on the fibreglass. Bow and stern sections contain foam buoyancy and beneath the foredeck are five watertight compartments. The effectiveness of the positive buoyancy was demonstrated in a tragic incident, shortly before we set sail from England. Motley One is OC 23; we saw No.21depart from Southampton, bound for Tokyo. During the first night out she was run down by a tanker, in bad weather off Portland Bill. Skipper Roger Bonnar was injured and his wife, asleep in the starboard cabin where the ship's bow struck, suffered a broken back. They were taken off by the ship and later transferred to hospital in the Isle of Wight by lifeboat, fortunately to recover in time. Karuna was abandoned. Three days later she was found by the Navy, still afloat, though completely waterlogged, with stores for three, months, ocean cruising gear and two diesel engines aboard.By the time we were able to set out it was December. With a new boat, a raw crew and no long-distance cruising experience, we made a timid beginning,day-sailing to France then coastwise, learning as we went.

Biscay in January gave Motley a severe test. Soon after rounding Ushant we experienced the most exhilarating sail she has ever provided. With a quartering Force 6 wind, under all but full sail, we spent an afternoon averaging nine knots, surging off wave tops at 12+. She has never done it since, perhaps because we've become progressively more laden, but maybe having too much sail up in too much wind had something to do with it. It says a lot for the boat though, that she did it, safely, in inexperienced hands. Several severe gales beset us in Biscay, the worst being reported as Force 10. With our inexperienced stomachs and taut nerves we didn't press on for long in Force 8, though the ketch rig does make it easy to balance the sail plan so that it is unnecessary to handle the wheel. As wind increases the first reduction is made by roller reefing the mains'l. I only do that once, down to the first batten; then the mains'l is taken down entirely. Two head sails, a yankee jib and a clubbed stays'l balance the full mizzen. With the wind at Force 8 it is still possible to keep the boat on course by using just the stays'l, balanced by the pendant reefed mizzen. At first I would heave to, using jib and mizzen but later with favourable drift, I spared the sails and lay a-hull. We found that Motley lays directly beam on to the wind and being light, on the water rather than in it, rises over the steepest waves. Occasionally, in Biscay, when 30ft waves were coming at us, a crest would break against the side, throwing spray over the roof and giving the boat a shunt sideways, sometimes. sufficient to throw things from the shelves. No waves ever crashed aboard and for the family life continued normally, with scheduled lessons for the children and full meals, cooked on a gymbal-less gas cooker, served on plates on the fiddle-less table. Two faults did become apparent before we reached Vigo, Spain. The joints, where the bridge section joins the hulls began to leak badly in the bows. A hard setting filler had been used in the joints and insufficient laminations had been used to cover them inside (easily remedied by the builders on subsequent craft). As the bows banged down, water was forced through the joints, into the buoyant bow sections causing them to get heavier and increase the pounding, and into internal cupboard. A lot of goods were ruined as water ran down to the bilges. These, five a side, are separate and shallow, easily baled or pumped dry. We use a manual diaphragm pump, with 25ft of hose, mounted in a cockpit locker. The second fault was in the steering gear which developed a bias to port. When we beached the boat in Spain I found the rudders inclined toward each other because the tiller arms, concealed in compartments under the stern deck, had bent under the strain of counteracting the big swells. From Spain to Madeira was a 700 mile beat, and we were often hove-to in wild conditions, taking 20 days for the passage. One gale blew Force 11 and continued for three days. Seeking shelter we sailed, beam-on to enormous waves, around into the lee of the Isles Desertas. There, for the first time I used a form of sea anchor: a 6in circumference warp, fastened fore and aft so that the 75ft bight trailed to windward. Buoyed in the centre to stay near the surface it seemed to reduce the number of crests that pounded Motley's side, and effectively reduced our drift (Fig 1). At last we were allowed to reach the Canary Isles and emerge into the sun and warmth. Sally and the girls had learnt to bear patiently with very rough waters, wild weather and' the frustration of delays, Motley had proved herself, we had confidence in her, she was home. The trepidation Sally felt stemmed from the extent of the Atlantic waters we had to cross to reach our objective, Antigua, in the West Indies. The rudders had stood the test from Spain, but I again had to recaulk the hull joints and put patches on cracks in the longitudinal struts of the bridge section, caused by flexing (Fig 2). Handicapped by costs, I had made little provision for trade wind running. Motley One had twin forestays, an extra masthead halyard, a second jib and a Genoa. In the ideal conditions of Southampton Water the two jibs had proved capable of driving the boat, lightly loaded and being trimmed to keep her before the wind, but I soon found that, laden, in choppy waters, they did not give enough drive. Determined not to be a slave to the wheel I experimented with a variety of sail configurations. With all working sails set closehauled, Motley will beat to windward, with the wheel unattended, amidships, holding a course 55 degrees off the true wind. Off the wind, until it is about 35° aft of the beam, she can be made to hold a course, without use of the wheel, by sail balancing. Any slight imbalance from the use of only one headsail, even a genoa, can be counteracted by setting a small amount of helm. There is sufficient friction in the linkage to the rudders to keep the wheel at whatever position is desired. Once the wind is around to the quarter if the mainsail is used the boat tries to head up into wind, excessive contrary rudder simply causes a gybe.

Figure 3, downwind, hands off. Mainsail broad off, jib hard in . . . easy sailing dead before

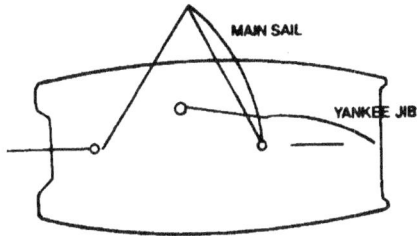

MAIN SAIL

YANKEE JIB

Figure 4, extra drive from second jib

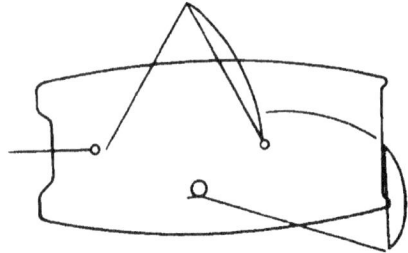

Figure 5, main boom used for genoa, balanced by jib well forward

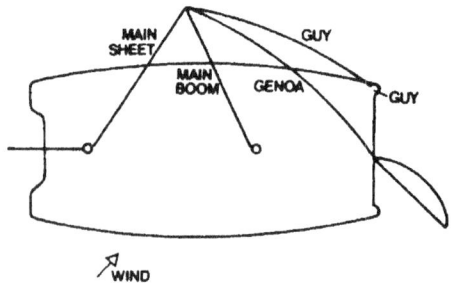

MAIN SHEET

MAIN BOOM

GUY

GENOA

GUY

WIND

Fig. 1

A-HULL

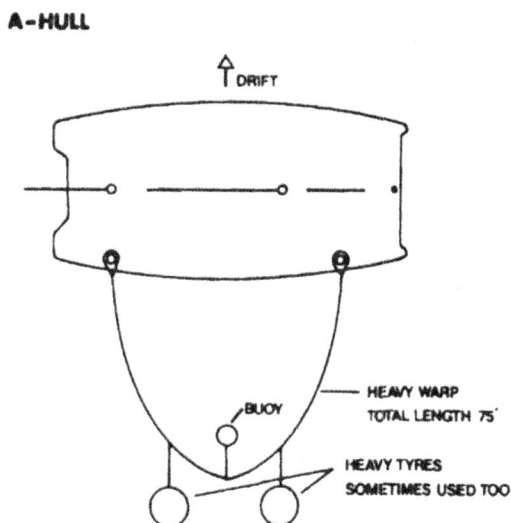

I found I could correct the tendency by using a jib sheeted flat and not using the mizzen(Fig 3). To provide additional drive I set the second jib opposite the main, boomed out with a whisker pole pivoted on the forestay (Fig 4). This worked well dead downwind, though if a gust or swell turned the bows far off course, the sails did not correct. Also, the head of the mains'! chaffed on the upper diamond stays so usually I took in a couple of rolls on the boom. Having no long spinnaker boom,I used the main boom to hold out the genoa when we had a quartering wind; setting a yankee well forward on the opposite side. (Fig 1). A six-day calm in mid-Atlantic, followed by light south westerlies, extended our crossing to 35 days and it was the end of April (1969) when we reached English Harbour, in Antigua.

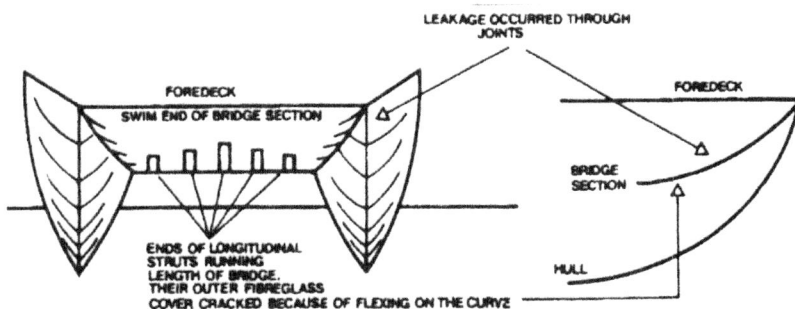

Throughout the year we stayed in Antigua we took more than 400 people sailing, many of them middle-aged Americans and Canadians who had never been out in a sailing boat before. A large proportion of these would never have tried the new experience if they could not, in our comings and goings, and from our daily family life aboard in full view see the tremendous advantages of a catamaran, its stability. With only 2ft draught and no keels or unprotected rudders to worry about, I could take Motley

right on to the beach to load and unload passengers over the bows. On the big foredeck there is room for four people to stretch out in the sun, or sit across under the pulpit, feet dangling inches above the backs of porpoises that often joined us to cavort between the hulls. We normally set a limit of eight passengers; if it became cool up for'ard as we beat back in the evening they could all sit in the cockpit, still leaving roomfor me to work helm and sails. I did it all myself, leaving Sally to look after the children and act as hostess. Motley being self steering, most of the time I also acted as barman. If it rained everyone could get inside. No heeling meant no holding on, freedom of movement for the guests and, of course, that their drinks, an important part of the proceedings, were safe. On a 30-footer!Two incidents did mar our stay. First I caused an explosive fire in the engine compartment by accidentally putting my foot on a fuel line while working on the engine as it was running. The fibreglass resisted the heat, and damage was confined to wiring and me. Later, returning after dark, I misjudged the distance offshore when approaching the hotel and stranded Motley on coral, wedged between rocks. The skegs underneath the rudders broke through the coral and, as the boat turned on the swell, one broke off, the associated rudder was torn off, and the other rudder, forced beyond its limits, sheared its tiller linkage. Through a worrying night, the children sent ashore, Sally and I turned Motley around, the tide range only one foot, and next day, after unloading all heavy gear by dinghy to the beach 200 yards away, we pulled our home off the rocks. The hulls were only scratched, but with no rudders we could not get to any harbour with facilities to haul us out. Friends in a construction company came to the rescue and we built a made-to-measure slipway on the beach and hauled Motley up with a tractor. Two weeks later, with new wooden rudders, she was relaunched by the muscle power of all the workmen off the site and a "One, two, three, push de man's boat" from the foreman. Our crewman had returned home.

Planning to continue westward we had to consider whether we could manage on our own. A cruise through the islands satisfied us that we could, and after provisioning at Grenada we set out to cross the Caribbean to Panama. The 420-mile first leg to Curacao, dead downwind in Force 3, took just four days. Shortly after we passed Aruba on the second stage a strong gale had us a-hull for two days. On the third day, the wind having eased somewhat, I set the two jibs, goose-winged, and stayed at the wheel. Going dead before the wind Motley was really moving, fast enough for the propeller to turn the engine, in gear; frequently surging as huge swells overtook us. In mid-afternoon we suddenly entered an area where a secondary swell was running down from the starboard, beam. One of the first of these caught Motley as she was perched on top of an overtaking crest and she slewed hard to port, broaching across the wind on the face of the next wave. Everything movable was thrown over to starboard, including the high seat I sat on at the wheel, but nothing carried away and there was sufficient way on for me to turn back on to course as the waves passed, leaving a blanket of foam 50 yards across laid out before us for over 100 yards. Passing through Panama, we emerged into the Pacific in August, the wrong time of year for our intended passage to the Galapagos. Light south-westerly winds and strong contrary currents proved too much for us. Unable to reach the "tortoise" islands and so go on from them southward, across the trade winds until we could turn in to our next destination Peru, we were forced to beat on down the South American coast. Sailing at 55° to light contrary winds always parallel to the coast, making 15° leeway and stemming the cold Peru current, Motley was in a motor-sailer's nightmare. After nine weeks at sea we finally put in at Paita, northern Peru, to reprovision and rest, before motoring most of the remaining 500 miles to Callao. Leaving after a stay of five months, we had an easy passage, "downhill", with wind and current to the Galapagos. Provisioned for six months, enough we hoped, to get us to New Zealand, with extra fuel and water, we were asking Motley to carry 2500 kilos! Instead of continuing, downwind to the Marquesas, we chose to reach, across the SE trades,to Easter Island, best day's run, 138 miles, then westward. Nearing Pitcairn we rode out the worst weather we have ever seen, in an intense depression. Well prepared, in open ocean, we had no qualms. Sleeping when the "eye" reached us, we were roused by hammer blows under the bridge section as the enormous waves, suddenly bereft of their driving force, crashed about in confusion. Crests washed across fore and aft decks or burst heavily against the side, but no solid water fell aboard. Within an hour the hurricane force winds resumed from exactly the opposite direction, driving Motley exactly sideways again. Some time later, when our tired sails were all damaged by furious squalls as we beat across the lagoon of the Gambler Islands we were driven right out of the pass again. With islands around for reference, I was able to accurately measure the sideways drift at two and a half knots, though dragging warp and tyres. That same night, to avoid being swept on to Temoe

Atoll, I had to reset the staysail. With wind and seas abeam Motley clawed forward, enough. The terylene sails, after almost daily use for two and a half years, constantly exposed to strong sunlight, had become rotten. The additional strain imposed by lack of heeling showed in failure of the clews; that of the mains'l splitting along the boom, those on the heads'ls tearing right off.

I have said little about speed, for Motley One's performance can not be taken as typical of the Oceanic class, because of the overload, and indifferent sails. Our best day's run, downwind, in the Atlantic, was 154 miles; reaching across the SE trades to Easter Island we bettered 130 miles several times. Generally though, in fair conditions, whatever the point of sailing we were happy if we exceeded 5 knots.

Here in New Zealand I have found considerable prejudice against catamarans. When trying to insure Motley for the most limited usage, I was told by insurance companies that they could not accept the risk, "multihulls are too unsafe". But in telling of Motley One's trials I have shown that cruising comfort can be found, on an even keel, with safety. It's time to recognise the fact, you conservative Kiwi keelermen, that catamarans can cope.

MORE TO READ

This collection of articles came about initially from the requirements of a contract with the British newspaper, The Daily Sketch,which was offered in the days before Motley One sailed from England. It was proposed that Sally Hope contribute writings that portrayed family life on a small sailing boat cruising Oceans. Unfortunately the newspaper foundered soon after and the material submitted was never used, many of the photographs, sent in on undeveloped film, were lost. The written material, illustrated by some photographs, presented in this short book, are a prelude to the publication of a fuller account of the Hope voyages.
The full story of the journey via Spain, Gran Canaria, across the Atlantic to Antigua, told in the new volume, 'MOTLEY ONE.', To Antigua.
The year spent there doing Day Chartering before going onward to Panama, is going to be presented in 'MOTLEY ONE', In the Caribbean.
    The tale of their travels in the Pacific, down to Peru, to the Galapagos Islands, down to Easter Island, across to Pitcairn, Mangareva, and on via Tahiti, to New Zealand, will be set out in 'MOTLEY ONE', In the Pacific.
    The daily journal written by Richard through his seven month, solo, non stop voyage from New Zealand to England is told in 'The Voyage Home'.

Printed in Great Britain
by Amazon